Under the Hawthorn Tree

THE GREAT IRI...

A Study Guide to the N...

IRENE BAR...

Introduction

Across the centuries of myth and legend in the oral tradition, folk culture and literature of Ireland, the hawthorn tree has long been associated with the supernatural. The hawthorn was the shrub around which the fairies were said to gather for their midnight revels. In rural tradition it has long been considered an omen of ill luck to damage or dig up a hawthorn tree. There are instances in the recent past of roads and motorways being realigned for fear of damaging an old hawthorn.

Marita Conlon-McKenna has used this powerful symbolism not only in the title *Under the Hawthorn Tree* but also in the setting of her famine novel in Ireland in the middle of the nineteenth century.

The potato crop has failed and famine stalks the land between 1845 and 1848. Three children, Eily, Michael and Peggy O'Driscoll, are left to fend for themselves when they are separated from their parents. Their baby sister has died and is buried beneath the hawthorn tree. In desperation, they set out on a perilous journey in search of their great-aunts, their last resort. Their journey is full of adventure and danger but eventually they reach their goal.

Apart from being a cracking good read, *Under the Hawthorn Tree* has proved to be popular with both teachers and pupils alike in the exploration of a wide variety of social and political issues in nineteenth-century Ireland. This Guide extends that inquiry and provides good opportunities for pupils to undertake a range of integrated and graded language and history activities.

The film treatment of *Under the Hawthorn Tree* was produced for Channel 4 by Kilkenny-based Young Irish Film Makers. It is Channel 4's first investment in a training-led film production process controlled entirely by children. They achieved remarkable results and C4 Schools is pleased to have backed them.

The O'Brien Press and Channel 4 Schools are interested in your comments on this Study Guide. You can e-mail them to Channel 4 Schools website at: **http://www.channel4.com/schools. Go to the Forum section and click on the *Under the Hawthorn Tree* topic.**

CONTENTS

First published 1998 by The O'Brien Press Ltd.
20 Victoria Road, Rathgar, Dublin 6, Ireland.
Tel. +353 1 4923333 Fax. +353 1 4922777
e-mail: books@obrien.ie website: http://www.obrien.ie
in association with Channel 4 Learning

Copyright for text, typesetting, layout © The O'Brien Press Ltd.

ISBN 0-86278-583-9

1 2 3 4 5 6 7 8 9 10
98 99 00 01 02 03 04 05 06

Typesetting, layout, design: The O'Brien Press
Editing: The O'Brien Press and Channel 4 Schools
Printing: Leinster Leader

DRAMA OUTLINE

The story is set in Ireland in the middle of the last century. The potato crop has failed and famine stalks the land. Three children, Eily, Michael and Peggy O'Driscoll, are left to fend for themselves when they are separated from their parents. In desperation, they set out on a perilous journey in search of their great-aunts, their last resort. The journey is full of adventure and danger but eventually the children reach their goal. **The film is in four episodes.**

Episode 1, Hunger, corresponds to book pages 1-26

Episode 2, On Their Own, to book pages 27-42

Episode 3, The Journey, to book pages 43-77

Episode 4, The Search, to book pages 78-150.

AIMS

To provide an opportunity to experience the pleasure of reading/watching an engaging and engrossing story.

To explore a wide variety of social and political issues of nineteenth-century Ireland.

To enable the students to undertake a range of integrated and graded language activities.

BEFORE VIEWING

Students should be encouraged to read the appropriate pages of text prior to viewing. If planning to read the book aloud to the class, allow one minute per page (more if pupils are reading aloud).

This book/film is set in Ireland, then part of the British Empire, in the middle of the *nineteenth century*. The country is in the grip of *famine* and the action centres around the plight of three children who embark on a *journey* of survival. Discuss these three central topics before viewing: nineteenth century, famine, journey.

Nineteenth Century

Brainstorm what the students know about life in the nineteenth century:

- from their family history (allowing 30 years per generation and working back from their own date of birth, let them calculate which of their relatives were alive in the last century).

- from the locality (what public buildings, statues, gravestones, landmarks, street furniture, houses, shops etc. were built in the last century?).

- from their knowledge of national and international history (what major events were taking place at that time?).

Famine

What does the word mean? What causes famine? Who is most vulnerable and why? Does it still occur? Where and why? What can we do?

Journey

Brainstorm books which tell the story of a journey. Explore the many types of journeys: sea, land, air, physical, emotional, spiritual, imagined, pilgrimages, quests, crusades, escapes, exiles, myths, legends, in different ages and places, unaccompanied, in small or large groups. Display findings.

THE GREAT IRISH FAMINE 1845-1848

The population of Ireland in 1841 was over 8 million. They lived on the potato, an abundant and nutritious vegetable, which didn't require much land to cultivate. Most people lived on tiny farms rented from landlords. Almost half of the farms were less than 5 acres (2 hectares). Living conditions were poor and there was always the threat of eviction for non-payment of rent. Workhouses were set up.

1845

Blight, a fungal disease, destroyed much of the potato crop. The Government imported maize, known as 'yellow meal' – initially people did not know how to cook it. Public Works Schemes were set up to provide employment so that people could earn money to buy food. Some landlords did their utmost to help their starving tenants, others evicted those who couldn't pay rent and pulled down their cabins. Some landlords lived outside the country and did nothing to help.

1846

The crop failed again. Soup-kitchens were set up by government agencies, private organisations and religious groups, and soup was given free. This was a new policy but government initiatives were totally inadequate. People were starving and disease was rampant – famine fever, typhus, dysentery and later cholera.

1847

This year was known as 'Black 47'. The early months were particularly cold and windy and, though the crop did not fail, supplies were low as people had had no seed potatoes to plant. People were desperate and those who could left the country for England and North America. People died on the roads, in the streets, in the cottages, in the fields. Direct government aid declined and the cost of famine relief fell to the Irish landlords. This led to greater pressure to evict pauper tenants.

1848

Blight returned again and many more died. But gradually conditions improved, though in 1870 the crop failed once again in the West of Ireland – but aid came quickly and the crisis was localised. The impact of the famine was felt for many years. The population declined by 2 million between the years 1845 and 1851. The Irish language declined. A pattern of emigration began. The inequity of land ownership led to the land war of 1879-1882.

EPISODE 1 – HUNGER

SUMMARY

The three main characters, Eily, Michael and Peggy O'Driscoll, are introduced at a point where famine is becoming widespread due to failure of the potato crop. Their parents, Margaret and John, work a small plot of land but when the potatoes are destroyed by blight John goes to seek work on a government relief scheme. We meet Mary Kate, a wise woman with healing powers, but even she cannot save their baby sister Bridget, who dies of fever at the end of the first episode.

NOTE TO TEACHERS

Some scenes in this episode may be upsetting for children who have recently been bereaved.

BEFORE VIEWING

Pupils to select one of the three characters to shadow during the viewing of the four episodes of this film. At the end of each episode pupils will be required to write an original journal entry through the eyes of the chosen character (to be written from the viewpoint of looking back over events which have occurred).

AFTER VIEWING

With pupils, summarise the episode orally. Questioning might be guided by the summary above.

WORKSHEET ACTIVITIES TABLE – AT A GLANCE

W/SHEET NO.	TITLE	ENGLISH	HISTORY	MEDIA STUDIES	SPHE/PSHE
1	Character Sketches	Character sketches/diary writing			
2	Beginnings	Opening paragraphs/ setting/ first impressions		Opening sequences/setting – compare novel and screenplay	
3	Everyday Life in Ireland in the 1840s	Period detail	Everyday life in the 1840s		Hygiene
4	Housing for Rich and Poor		Housing in the nineteenth century		Living conditions
5	Crop Failure, Hunger, Famine		Crop failure, famine, population decline		Diet
6	Disease and Death	Haiku	Famine diseases and burial		
7	The Hawthorn Tree in Folklore	Hawthorn as an image / descriptive writing	Folklore and the hawthorn tree		

CHARACTER SKETCHES

EILY

MICHAEL

PEGGY

1 In the boxes above write adjectives which describe the three main characters. Decorate the frames above.

2 Journal entry: On a separate sheet, write a journal entry for the character you are shadowing. The title might be, for example, 'May 1846, the day we buried Bridget'. You might like to complete these sentences:

> Today I feel ...
> I wish ...
> My mother ...
> My father ...
> The only good thing ...

Now continue on your own.

Or you may prefer to structure your journal entry in your own way. Keep this piece of writing carefully. Write a

journal entry directly after each of the other three episodes.

3 Make a 3D frame using materials of your choice, eg pasta shapes, fluff, stones, shells. Draw a portrait of the character you have chosen and mount it in your frame.

4 Read diary accounts of other events. Check out the following:

The Diary of a Young Girl, Anne Frank (Puffin Modern Classics, 1998, ISBN 014-03856-30)

Sisters ... No Way!, Siobhán Parkinson (The O'Brien Press, 1997, ISBN 0-86278-495-6)

The Life and Loves of Zoe T. Curley, Martin Waddell (Walker Books, 1997, ISBN 0-7445-4166-2)

The Secret Diary of Adrian Mole, age 13¾, Sue Townsend (Methuen, 1984, ISBN 0-413-53790-0)

BEGINNINGS

First impressions last.
The first few paragraphs of a book, or the first few scenes of a film,
must introduce the characters and set the scene
and they must do so in a way that grabs your attention or else you may switch off.

Here is what Siobhán Lyons, co-director of the film *Under the Hawthorn Tree,* had to say about the opening sequence and the potato scene:

THE OPENING SEQUENCE

'The pre-credit scenes of the film had a number of jobs to do: firstly, they had to introduce the main characters to the audience, and secondly they had to create a certain tension before the final climax, ie, the news of the potato blight. In order to create a mood of apprehension the scenes are choppy and no-one is sure what exactly is going on until the running boy bursts into the schoolroom. The contrast between the quiet of the classroom and the energy of the running boy is another way of confusing and misleading the audience.'

THE POTATO SCENE

'Once the children reach their home after hearing of the disaster, they behold the pathetic sight of their father, on his knees in the mud, looking sorrily at his potato patch. They run to survey the damage; Michael tries to salvage the last of the potatoes. Eily, realising what has happened, seems dazed and Peggy, in total confusion, watches her father and looks to Eily for an answer. This is a sorry scene – it is the beginning of the end for the three O'Driscolls. The sudden scream of their mother adds even more panic to the scene and the audience have more sympathy for the family. The final words, before the roll of opening credits, are spoken by the wise old woman, Mary Kate: "Now surely, the hunger will come." These words are a signal for what is to come.'

1 View the opening sequence of the film again just as far as the opening credits. Does this sequence achieve what the directors intended it should?

2 Read the first two-and-a-half pages of the book. In what ways are the book and the film similar?

3 In what ways are they dissimilar? Which do you prefer? Give reasons for your answer.

READ IT AND WEEP

The Edward Bulwer Lytton Prize is awarded annually to the author of the worst possible opening line of a book. The prize has become so successful that Penguin Books have published a number of books containing entries submitted from all over the world. Here is one:

'With a curvaceous figure that Venus would have envied, a tanned, unblemished oval face framed with lustrous thick, brown hair, deep azure-blue eyes fringed with long black lashes, perfect teeth that vied for competition, and a small straight nose, Marilee had a beauty that defied description.'

Makes you weep.

4 Look at the opening paragraph of three books of your choice. What do they tell you about: the setting? the characters? the plot?

5 Write an opening paragraph of your own *or* select one of those chosen above and write on ...

EVERYDAY LIFE IN IRELAND IN THE 1840s

What information can you find out from the book and film about everyday life in the last century?

1 Record your findings below (see Medicine example).

2 Plan a research project on everyday life in Ireland or Britain in the nineteenth century. You might like to divide into groups and examine the topics below. Other topics you might explore: children, work.

TOPIC	PAGE OF BOOK	SCENE FROM FILM
Housing/bedding	pp. 9, 11, 14	
Food/fuel	pp. 11, 12, 13, 15, 16, 19, 20, 21	
Clothes	pp. 9, 10, 22	
Medicine	p. 13 Mary Kate had cures – goose grease to rub on Bridget's chest	Mary Kate collects herbs, has bottles and jars in her window, has herbs drying in her house, has the name of being a witch, recycles jars, shows doubt in the ability of her cure to heal the strange new sickness
Washing/hygiene	pp. 12, 13	
Recreation (visiting, storytelling, swimming, fishing, playing)	pp. 17, 19	
Education	p.10	

WORKSHEET 3

TEACHER'S STUDY GUIDE

Under the Hawthorn Tree
The Great Irish Famine
A Study Guide to the Novel and Film

DETAILS
£4.95 pb
ISBN 0-86278-583-9
Trim size: A4
Age Group: 10+

Published with Channel 4 Learning, the schools division of the major British TV channel who will screen the film in March 1999.

- Packed with ideas for classroom use of this best-selling novel and the film based on it, this study guide will be invaluable to both primary and second-level teachers. Activities relate to language, literature history and social studies and are set to different levels of competence.

- Designed to fulfill requirements of the new curricula for the Republic of Ireland, Northern Ireland, England, Scotland and Wales.

- Marita Conlon-McKenna is a major award-winning author and this novel has broken all records for sales in Ireland. It has been translated into Japanese, Danish, Dutch, French, German, Swedish.

- Marita Conlon-McKenna's awards for *Under the Hawthorn Tree* include: The International Reading Association Award, The Reading Association of Ireland Award, Osterreichischer Kinder- und Jugendbuchpreis.

- Famine is a major universal issue of continuing importance and relevance - and is part of the curriculum in Britain and Ireland.

NOVELS

Under the Hawthorn Tree ISBN 0-86278-206-6 £4.99 PB
Wildflower Girl ISBN 0-86278-283-X £4.50 PB
Fields of Home ISBN 0-86278-509-X £4.99 PB

VIDEO

Under the Hawthorn Tree VIDEO
4x20 MINUTE EPISODES £14.95

The film was made by Young Irish Film Makers, backed by RTE (Irish television) and by Channel 4

ORDER FORM

Please send me the items as marked
___ *Under the Hawthorn Tree* @ £4.99   ___ *Wildflower Girl* @ £4.50
___ *Under the Hawtorn Tree Study Guide* @ £4.95   ___ *Fields of Home* @ £4.99
___ *Under the Hawthorn Tree Video Cassette* @ £14.95
I enclose cheque/postal order for £ . . . .(+£1.00 P&P per unit, over 10 items post free)
OR please charge my credit card___ Access/Mastercard___ Visa

Card Number __ __ __ __   __ __ __ __   __ __ __ __   __ __ __ __

Expiry Date__ __ / __ __

Name. . . . . Tel: . . . .

Address . . . .

. . . .

Please send orders to:

Ireland
THE O'BRIEN PRESS
20 Victoria Road, Dublin 6
Tel: +353 1 4923333
Fax: +353 1 4922777

Britain
CHANNEL 4 SCHOOLS
PO Box 100, Warwick
CV34 6TZ, UK
Tel: 01926 436444
Fax: 01926 436446
Email: sales@schools.channel4.co.uk

Trade Orders
GILL & MACMILLIAN DISTRIBUTION
Goldenbridge Industrial Estate, Inchicore, Dublin 8
Tel: +353 1 4531005
Fax: +353 1 4541688

HOUSING FOR RICH AND POOR

The village above is the type of village in which many people lived in the nineteenth century. The houses were one-roomed mud cabins, thatched with straw, potato stalks or sods of turf. There was one door, no windows and frequently the houses were shared with animals – cows, calves and pigs. Potatoes were grown on small plots of land beside the cabin.

The inhabitants might have worked as labourers for tenant farmers. The tenant farmer's house might have been large and comfortable, with windows and chimneys. He would have had a farmyard, with outhouses for the animals. He would have owned a horse and trap for transport. These farmers rented their land from the landlords who lived in houses like those below.

The worst off were the wandering labourers who did seasonal work for farmers when they could get it, otherwise they begged or stole. They lived in temporary hovels along the side of the road.

1 Make four sketches which show the differing levels of prosperity of the people: a labourer's hovel, a cottier's cabin, a tenant farmer's house, a landlord's mansion.

2 Which houses in your area were built in the nineteenth century or even earlier? Were they the homes of the rich or the poor? Sketch or photograph them.

3 Mount a classroom display of local pre-twentieth century buildings.

4 You might like to make a model of the O'Driscoll cottage with *papier maché*.

CROP FAILURE, HUNGER, FAMINE

Famine was not uncommon in Ireland prior to the Great Famine (1845-1848). The famine of 1740-41 may have been as serious but evidence is scant – foreign travellers spoke of the extreme poverty of the Irish at that time.

- In 1800 there were 5 million people in Ireland. By 1840 the population had increased to over 8 million. Farms were subdivided into smaller and smaller portions so people were depending on very small areas of land to support them. Increasingly, potatoes became the staple diet as they were filling, nutritious and did not need much land for cultivation.

- The famine was caused by continuous failure of the potato crop due to a fungal disease (thought to have come from South America via Europe) called blight. This disease still attacks potatoes today but farmers spray their crops to control it.

- Over a million people died of disease and starvation. Over a million emigrated to Britain or America.

The potato plant

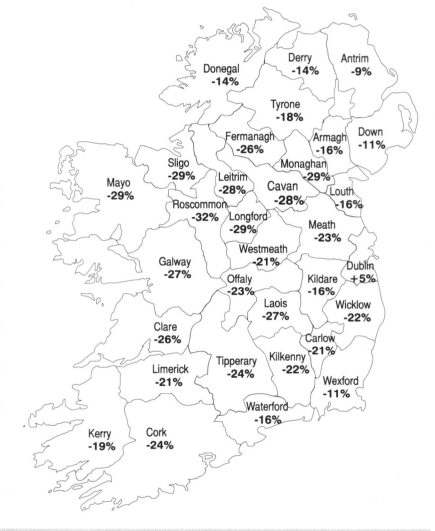

This map shows the changes in population brought about by the famine.

1 Colour the counties with a decrease of between 0 and 10% purple

2 Colour the counties with a decrease of between 11% and 20% red

3 Colour the counties with a decrease of between 21% and 30% blue

4 Colour the counties with a decrease in excess of 30% black

5 Which area of Ireland was worst affected?

6 In your opinion, why did the population of Dublin increase?

7 What advantages do you think people living by the sea had?

The potato was the staple diet of the Irish people in the last century. This table shows the typical daily diet of a labouring man.

BREAKFAST 4.5lbs potatoes, 1 pint of milk
DINNER 4.5lbs potatoes and herrings when milk could not be obtained
SUPPER 4.5lbs potatoes, 1 pint of milk

8 If an average potato weighs 200g, calculate how many potatoes a labourer would consume each day (1lb = 454g).

9 Is this a balanced diet? Give reasons for your answer.

DISEASE AND DEATH

- Many people died of disease as well as starvation.

- Dysentery, typhoid and later cholera wiped out hundreds of thousands of people.

- So many died that bodies were often carted uncoffined to mass burial places.

- As in any famine, the old and the young, being the most vulnerable, were the first to die.

- In all, over one million people died.

Read pages 21-26.

1 In your workbook, record how the main characters reacted to Bridget's death. Write your notes under the headings: Mother, Eily, Peggy, Michael, Dan Collins, Kitty Collins. Record how they prepared for her funeral.

2 What circumstances surrounding the burial added to the mother's grief?

3 The funeral in the picture above took place near Skibbereen, Co. Cork, one of the areas to suffer most during the famine. Look at the clothing, transport, mourners, coffin. Why do you think burial scenes like this took place in a country which usually showed great respect for the dead?

4 Interview old people you know about the practices surrounding death, burial and mourning in their childhood.

5 Find out about a wake, or about the banshee.

The following books may prove helpful: *Irish Wake Amusements*, Seán Ó Súilleabháin (Mercier Press, 1979, ISBN 0-85342-1455); *Death Customs*, Lucy Rushton (Wayland, 1995, ISBN 0-75021-6662), *A Pocket Book of the Banshee*, Patricia Lysaght (The O'Brien Press, 1998, ISBN 0-86278-501-4).

HAIKU

A haiku is a three-line poem, the first line having 5 syllables, the second line 7 syllables and the third line 5 syllables. Write a haiku entitled 'For Bridget', or 'The Hawthorn Tree'.

Here is a sample haiku:

> **A bitter morning**
> **sparrows sitting together**
> **without any necks**

EPISODE 1 – HUNGER

WORKSHEET 6

THE HAWTHORN TREE IN FOLKLORE

According to folklore, the lone hawthorn was the shrub around which the fairies gathered for their midnight revels. Even today it is considered bad luck to dig up a hawthorn. (It is said that the real curse placed upon the failed de Lorean car plant in Belfast came when an old whitethorn was cleared to make way for it!)

HAWTHORN Latin name: *crataegus monogyna* Irish name: *sceach gheal*

In this extract from the poem, 'The Fairies' by William Allingham, there is a warning not to interfere with the fairies!

THE FAIRIES
 (A Child's Song)
William Allingham

Up the airy mountain,
Down the rushy glen,
We daren't go a-hunting
For fear of little men;
Wee folk, good folk,
Trooping all together;
Green jacket, red cap,
And white owl's feather!

By the craggy hill-side,
Through the mosses bare,
They have planted thorn-trees
For pleasure here and there.
Is any man so daring
As dig one up in spite,
He shall find their sharpest thorns
In his bed at night.

An extract from
'Poet's Chair' by Seamus Heaney

My father's ploughing one, two, three, four sides
Of the lea ground where I sit all-seeing
At centre field, my back to the thorn tree
They never cut.

William Allingham (1824-1889): born Ballyshannon, Co. Donegal; editor, playwright and poet.

Seamus Heaney (b. 1939): born in Derry; awarded the Nobel Prize for Literature in 1995.

1 The hawthorn is an image which is used often in the book and film. It is referred to on pages 24, 117 and 150. Read these pages and record the purpose of the hawthorn image at that particular point of the story.

2 Do you think *Under the Hawthorn Tree* is an appropriate title? Give reasons for your answer. Can you think of alternative titles?

3 Why not try to find out about hawthorn tree traditions in your area and e-mail them to Channel 4 Schools website: http://www.channel4.com/schools. Go to the Forum section and click on the *Under the Hawthorn Tree* topic.

'*In early summer, right now, it comes to its sumptuous best, when it not merely turns our fields into rolling wolds of white, but of roseate and golden tints too, well beyond the mastery of any painter's brush, and the air is filled with the sweet marzipan fragrance of the blossom.*'
Kevin Myers, *The Irish Times*, 30 May 1998

Here is a wonderful description of hawthorn in full bloom. It tells us not only what the hawthorn looks like but what it smells like and hints at what it might taste like. 'Wold' means an expanse of open country.

4 Look up the meaning of the following adjectives: sumptuous, roseate, marzipan.

5 The use of carefully chosen adjectives adds greatly to the impact of your writing, especially if you are describing something. Write a descriptive passage about your favourite place. Before you start, list suitable adjectives; get help from a thesaurus.

EPISODE 2 – ON THEIR OWN

SUMMARY

Margaret goes to the village to exchange a dress and shawl for some food. The village is devastated by famine, houses boarded up, whole families dead or emigrated, people starving. She learns that the roadworks are about 20 miles away and hopes that her husband John might be there. Meanwhile, the children entertain themselves by performing a play about their great-aunts, Lena and Nano, about whom their mother has often told them stories. An old woman and her son call to the house but Michael's quick thinking sends them away. Margaret returns with food but shortly afterwards leaves the family to try to find John.

BEFORE VIEWING

Ask the pupils to remember to focus on the character they are shadowing and whose journal they are keeping. In particular, ask them to note their character's behaviour:

• **during their play**

• **when they are frightened**

• **when they are faced with great loss.**

AFTER VIEWING

With the pupils, summarise the episode using the summary above to guide your questioning. Ask them to write the journal entry entitled 'The day Mother went away'.

WORKSHEET ACTIVITIES TABLE – AT A GLANCE

W/SHEET NO.	TITLE	MEDIA STUDIES	ENGLISH	HISTORY	SPHE / PSHE
8	Home Alone/Follies		Dictionary research	Buildings/artefacts	Parenting
9	Lost Languages		Influences on language/dialects	Celtic languages	Terms of endearment
10	Saying Goodbye	Creating a drama Writing a screenplay			
11	Before and After the Famine/Film Episodes	Identify film episodes	Group discussion	Famine destruction	
12	Public Relief Works		Historical record	Oral sources	

HOME ALONE

This is the advice Margaret O'Driscoll gave her children before she went to the village:

- **Keep the fire going**
- **Get some water in**
- **Stay indoors**
- **Keep the door on the latch**

1 Give the reasons behind each piece of advice.

2 What advice would your mother give you if you were home alone? Give reasons for each piece of advice.

CIRCLE TIME

3 Form a circle in the classroom. Each person in turn is given the opportunity to speak on the topic: **Home Alone**.

Move clockwise around the circle.

The speaker holds a ruler, and only the person with the ruler may speak. You may recount your own experiences or offer opinions.

FOLLIES

As part of the Public Relief Scheme some landlords had 'follies' built on their lands. According to the Oxford English Dictionary a folly is 'a building erected for no definite purpose; a costly structure apparently built for fantastic reasons, or a useless and generally foolish building erected in the grounds of a wealthy eccentric'.

A folly could be a **grotto**, an **obelisk**, a **column**, a **sham castle**, a **gazebo**, a **hermitage**, a **tower**, a **temple**, a **gate**, a **lodge** or a **bridge**. Many were eccentric in design.

Here is an illustration of Connolly's Folly in Co. Kildare. It was erected by Mrs. Connolly, widow of William Connolly who was Speaker in the Irish House of Commons in the early eighteenth century. It is an obelisk 70 feet high, designed by German-born Richard Castle who came to Ireland in 1729. Castle put a narrow staircase in the piers of the Connolly Folly so that a person could climb up as high as the highest archway where fantastic views could be had of counties Kildare and Dublin.

Follies were sometimes built for the sole purpose of creating employment.

4 Design your own folly and give details of building materials, dimensions and location.

5 This folly has been called both the ugliest building in Ireland and the one real piece of architecture in Ireland! What do you think?

LOST LANGUAGES

Margaret uses many terms of affection when talking to her children,
some in the Irish language.
A stór: darling (pronounced: 'a store')
A ghile: beloved (pronounced 'a gillah')

1 What might an adult call you, other than your first name,
if they were feeling affectionate towards you?
2 Brainstorm the subject with your classmates and fill in the wall of endearment words below.
How many community/minority languages are used by members of your class?
3 Display your findings on a class chart.

Three indigenous languages have died out in Great Britain and Ireland during the past 225 years: Cornish (c.1775), Norn, the Norse language of Shetland (c.1880) and Manx (1974).

Four ancient indigenous minority languages remain: Welsh, Irish, Scots Gaelic and Channel Island French.

4 Do you know any family where any one of these four languages is the normal language of the home?

5 Suggest reasons why these languages are in decline.

6 Identify and list concerns about the fact that some languages have died out and others are in decline.

7 What do you think can be done to save them?

8 In the nineteenth century parents often supported the National Schools policy to promote English, as you can see in the extract opposite. Why did the father behave like this? Why was the punishment administered at school? Discuss.

THE TALLY STICK

'The children gathered round to have a look at the stranger, and one of them, a little boy about eight years of age, addressed a short sentence in Irish to his sister but, meeting the father's eye, he immediately cowered back, having, to all appearance, committed some heinous fault. The man called the child to him, said nothing, but drawing forth from its dress a little stick, commonly called a screen or tally, which was suspended by a string round the neck, put an additional notch in it with his penknife. Upon our enquiring into the cause of this proceeding, we were told that it was done to prevent the child speaking Irish; for every time he attempted to do so a new nick was put in his tally, and when these amounted to a certain number, summary punishment was inflicted on him by the schoolmaster.'

Sir William Wilde, 1853

SAYING GOODBYE

Here is an extract from the screenplay by the Young Irish Film Makers.
It was adapted from Marita Conlon-McKenna's book.
I Divide into groups of four and act out these two scenes.

Outside the house the children are playing. Margaret comes up the lane. She stops and watches her children at play. We see her face as she watches. The children play in slow motion. She is storing up this memory to sustain her on the road. Then she moves forward and calls each by name.

Margaret: Eily! Michael! Peggy! Come inside.

She walks straight through the garden and into the house. Eily and Michael look at each other and follow her in. Peggy runs after them.

CUT TO

Inside the house. The children troop in and look at Margaret. She is moving around the house packing some food into a bag. The children look at each other again.

Eily: Mammy ... Is anything wrong?

Margaret: I am going to find your father.

The children are shocked.

Michael: Isn't Daddy coming home?

Margaret: I don't know. It's been over four weeks now and no word. I have to go to the works and find out what has happened. He may be sick.

Eily: How long will you be away?

Margaret: It will be like the time I went to the village, but it may take a day or two.

Eily: Oh Mammy, a day or two?

Margaret: We have nothing left to trade or sell, the little food we have will run out soon ... How will we survive without help?

Michael: Mammy, please don't go!

Margaret: Please don't make it any harder for me. I have to do this.

Michael: Sorry, Mammy.

Peggy is looking from Eily to Michael to try and understand what is going on.

Margaret: There is enough to eat. Dan and Kitty will keep an eye on you.

Eily: Don't worry about us, Mammy. We'll be good. Just bring back Daddy to us.

She grabs her heavy shawl. She hugs each one in turn.

Margaret: Eily, you must take my place now. Michael, the man of the house and Peggy, my baby ... God keep you safe.

Peggy won't let her go. As Margaret tries to leave, Peggy is screaming and holding on to her. Eily and Michael finally manage to drag her off. They have to hold her by the waist and Margaret leaves and walks off down the lane. They are alone.

FADE OUT

2 How does this extract from the screenplay differ from the same scene in the book? (See pages 41 and 42.)

3 Do you think Margaret is irresponsible for leaving the children on their own? Give reasons for your answer.

4 In the book, find the sequence where the children meet up with Joseph T. Lucey (the beginning of the second paragraph on page 78 to 'Kineen it was then' on page 79). Write the screenplay for this sequence.

BEFORE AND AFTER THE FAMINE

Read pages 34 and 36-37. They provide a stark contrast between days
of relative prosperity before the famine and the devastation of the mid-1840s.

1 Restore the drawing of the village below to its pre-famine condition. Add people, animals etc.

FILM EPISODES

2 Which events in the story are portrayed in these stills from the film?

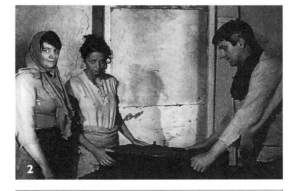

1
2
3

4 Discussion: Compare and contrast the feelings
of the characters in the three scenes.

EPISODE 2 – ON THEIR OWN

PUBLIC RELIEF WORKS 1846

- Government employment schemes were set up to enable starving people to buy food. This was in keeping with the ideas of the time that food should not be given free as this would encourage idleness and would interfere with the normal channels of trade.

- From October 1846 landlords were allowed to sponsor improvements on their own properties. This had the added bonus for the landlords of ensuring that their tenants could pay their rent on time and in cash.

- By the spring of 1847, 750,000 people were engaged in Public Relief Works. That same year the Government withdrew funding from the scheme, declaring it a waste of money.

ORAL SOURCES

Pádraig Ó Seaghdha, Fearann tSeáin, Castlegregory, Co. Kerry
The principal local relief scheme was the building of boundary walls on the mountains. The men employed were the able-bodied poor of the parish and the pay was fourpence a day, the men to find their own food. As I write I can see nine or ten miles of dry stone wall on the face of Binn Ós Gaoith. These run up to a height of 2,000 feet on the mountain side and enclose land which is not worth 4d. an acre.

John O'Reilly, a farmer, Glenville, Co. Cork, who heard it from his father, 1826-1906
The government grant for the relief scheme '46-47 was, we are told, £100,000. This was to relieve suffering humanity but the greater part was used up by clerks and commissioners. It was mainly the opening up of new roads through waste places and never used afterwards. I have estimated the amount of roadway as twelve and a half miles but it was more, as in travelling near where these roads were made, I find that branches from here and there lead to nowhere. When the poor starving men heard the 'good' news of a big sum of money being spent on works, they left the farmers in the lurch and applied for jobs. The result was that the farmer was not able to till his lands as heretofore, and the result was that the farmers became poor themselves.

Tomás Ó Ceallaigh, b.1860, a farmer, Caherea, Ennis, Co. Clare
Under the heading of local relief schemes comes the case of one of the landlords, Lord George Quinn, owner of the townland of Ballymorris. At the Government's request he employed a staff of from between 15 to 20 men. They were employed in different ways, some being engaged in the erection of three large two-storied houses in different parts of the parish, all in prominent positions. For example, one was built on high ground in Ballymorris overlooking the Shannon; another facing the railway and the third almost right on the summit of Cratloe Hills, the idea being to

show what was being done to relieve the conditions of some of the tenants at least. Other parts of the property were drained and fenced, in one case a farm of considerable size in those days had no less than 27 gates here and there through it. It was not all charity however as four percent was added to the rent.

Brigid Keane, Ennel View Terrace, Mullingar, Co. Westmeath
The 'whip-up', as they called the ganger, watched them all the time while he walked around cracking his whip. If a man showed any slackness or weakness at all he was knocked off at once. There was always plenty of men waiting around to get work. There might be a hundred men sitting on the boundary to see if any man would drop out. If the labourer was not able to do a certain amount of  work every day, he was knocked out of employment. Some men had to walk four or five miles daily to their work, or even farther.

Felix Kernan, b.1859, a farmer, Drumakill, Castleblayney, Co. Monaghan
Several local relief schemes were organised during the famine. New roads were made and fields and bogs drained. Churches and bridges were also built.

Michael Gorman, b.1868, Doontrusk, Carrowbeg, Westport, Co. Mayo
Subscriptions were made up all over England and Scotland and in other countries and it was estimated that the amount collected would give £5 to every family in Ireland. Many families got none of it. Relief works were started but no-one was allowed to work except those who had cards saying they were entitled to do so, and officials, gangers, timekeepers etc., got most of the money.

1 What work was carried out by the Relief Works? Make a list.

CLASS DISCUSSION
2 Who benefited most from the Relief Works: the poor? the landlord? others?

EPISODE 3 – THE JOURNEY

SUMMARY

The landlord's agent instructs the children to go to the workhouse as they have no means of support. They decide to go to Castletaggart to search for the great-aunts. With the help of Mary Kate, they escape from the workhouse group. They set out on their journey, full of excitement. The going is difficult and becomes more so when Michael injures his leg. Peggy is very upset when Michael kills a baby rabbit for food. However, later she eats it with relish!

BEFORE VIEWING

Ask the pupils to pay particular attention to the contribution of each child to their survival on the journey.

AFTER VIEWING

Frame questions to elicit a summary of the episode using the summary above as a guide. Ask the pupils to write their third journal entry entitled 'On the Road'.

WORKSHEET ACTIVITIES TABLE – AT A GLANCE

W/SHEET NO.	TITLE	ENGLISH	HISTORY	SPHE / PSHE
13	The Family Tree		Family history	
14	Starvation		Oral history	Alternative food sources
15, 16	Workhouses Newry Workhouse	Reading a plan	Documentary evidence/social welfare	Punishment
17	Folk Medicine	Using IT		Folk cures/use of plants
18	Landlords	Discussion and reading	The landlord system examined	

THE FAMILY TREE

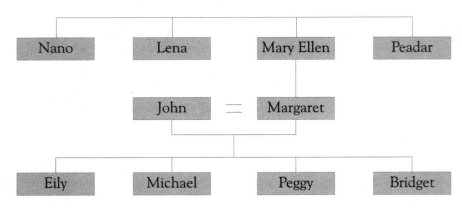

THE O'DRISCOLL FAMILY TREE

| Nano | Lena | Mary Ellen | Peadar |

| John | = | Margaret |

| Eily | Michael | Peggy | Bridget |

MY FAMILY TREE

---

1 Look at the O'Driscoll family tree. What relation was Peadar to Margaret? What relation was Michael to Lena? What relation was John to Mary Ellen? What relation was Eily to Mary Ellen?

2 Draw up your own family tree in the frame above, going back as far as you can on both your mother's and father's side. Start with yourself, add your brothers and sisters, and build back from there.

STARVATION

The children had little food to bring with them so they ate what they could find as they went along: wild strawberries, edible roots and a rabbit. With the meal, potatoes and milk they had, this, while it lasted, formed a balanced diet.

When the potato crop failed, people had no adequate substitute for this nutritious vegetable and malnutrition caused diseases such as anaemia, swollen and bleeding gums, painful joints, diarrhoea, itching and scaling of the skin, inflammation of the mouth, damaged sight leading to blindness.

> Read the extracts on this page and list the foods eaten when the potato crop failed.

Indian meal (maize)

ORAL SOURCES

Thomas O'Flynn, John Melody, Attymass, Ballina, Co. Mayo
Rabbits, hares and wild fowl were caught by having rights to hunt, the flesh was used and their soup, mixed with Indian meal, was considered excellent. Bull calves sold for half a crown and were not kept. They were slaughtered for food. Sheep provided most of the meat used and sheep stealing was common. Pigs were reared on a small scale and disappeared altogether when the potatoes failed. Goats were plentiful on the mountains and were practically wiped out for food during the Famine.

Seán Ó Beirne, Malin, Inishowen, Co. Donegal
They used all the usual foods to be found along the shore: dulse, sloak, famanach, wilks, barnacles, braillins, aghaus, cockles [dulse and famanach are seaweed, the rest are shellfish]. And dulaman. This dulaman is a growth somewhat like carageen moss or as they call it here in Inishowen 'crothar' and is not edible until after the first severe frost in Winter. It is not left to bleech like carageen but can be cooked [boiled] immediately after being pulled. It has to be boiled for two or three hours.

Mrs Fitzsimons, b.1875, Sheepstown, Delvin, Co. Westmeath
The people used to gather the leaves of the dandelions and boil them. Then they strained the water off and made gruel by putting meal into the water. They used to make drinks from the holly berries too.

John Treanor, b.1870, a retired scutcher, Forkhill, Co. Armagh
The people had to live on brawlum. It was a handful of meal and a head of cabbage. It was yellow meal though, you know, and maybe a dumpling if they had a fistful of flour. It was made anont of the butcher [made without any meat]. There was no meat in them days.

Seaghan Mac Cártha, b.1893, national teacher, An Bóthar Buí, Newmarket, Co. Cork
She [Máire] lived on herbs and turnips during the period after her husband died. She ate caisearbhán [dandelions], samha [sorrel, sour dock], nettles, turnips and anything she could find. Poor people could be seen crawling along the ditches looking for herbs, and their mouths were green from the leaves they were eating. Poor Máire's mouth was often green, but she lived through it all. She helped to nurse me and was a very decent soul. May the heavens be her bed.

Seán Ó Duinnshleibhe, Glenville, Fermoy, Co. Cork
In winter, men, women and children would be seen stalking through a turnip field where grew the turnips, to pick up any root of those vegetables left in the ground. In extreme hunger the children used eat grass.

Seán Ó Duinnshleibhe, Glenville, Fermoy, Co. Cork
They had no food for the cattle save hay alone, but none for the hens. The hens did not lay for the want of food, and then they became less and less until there were none. They had been killed and eaten.

Hugh Byrne, b.1915, Blindennis, Hacketstown, Co. Carlow
His father told him that a hungry man used to draw blood from the first thing he'd meet with. One man attacked a fox but he was so weak the fox snapped at him and took his arm off. Half the population died from hunger and were buried in the ditches.

P. Lennon, b.1900, Crossbridge, Co. Wicklow
People ate sycamore seeds. There were two kinds of haws they used eat, but one kind was poisonous. Many died from eating the latter because they didn't know the difference.

WORKHOUSES

In 1839 Ireland was divided into 130 districts called Poor Law Unions. Each Union was to have its own workhouse to accommodate the destitute of the area.

- These were harsh places where families were split up by age and gender. Food was basic, fever rampant and discipline strict.

- In the winter of 1846, around 2,500 people died each week in the workhouses.

- In 1847 Lord John Russell's government ended government relief of any sort and the burden of funding fell to the local landlords.

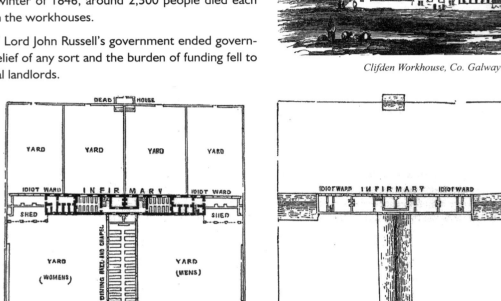

Clifden Workhouse, Co. Galway

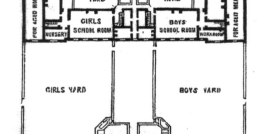

GROUND FLOOR.

FIRST FLOOR.

STUDY THESE PLANS AND ANSWER THESE QUESTIONS

1 How many workhouses were established in Ireland by 1846, the year in which *Under The Hawthorn Tree* is set?

2 What do you think happened in the hall of the workhouse?

3 Why are there two small front yards beyond the hall?

4 What was directly over the girls' schoolroom?

5 Which side of the building did the girls and women inhabit?

6 Where were the very sick accommodated?

7 What, do you think, was the purpose of the four small yards at the back of the buildings?

8 Why, do you think, was there such strict segregation of the sexes?

NEWRY WORKHOUSE

Public Record Office of Northern Ireland

EXTRACT FROM THE OFFENCES AND PUNISHMENT BOOK OF NEWRY WORKHOUSE, 1851-5.

The maintenance of discipline in Newry workhouse was notoriously difficult, due to overcrowding and to lack of harmony between the over-worked officers of the workhouse and the Board of Guardians. The master and matron were assaulted. Discipline was a matter often referred to in the master's reports to the guardians, whereas in most other Unions in Ulster it was apparently not pressing enough to be considered worthy of notice. This general situation may explain the severity of some of the punishments.

At an enquiry into indiscipline on 6 April 1850, the master explained his method of punishing by producing 'a leathern taws', which he said he used in preference to a ratan or rod, because he considered it less severe.

PUNISHMENT AT NEWRY

Twenty-nine women at the mill	Neglecting and refusing to work	1851 24th July	Dinner and supper milk stopped
Owen Trainor	Stealing onions	1st September	Flogged
James Acheson	Going to town without permission	14th February 1852	6 hours in lock-up
James Close	Refractory conduct	14th February 1852	6 hours in lock-up
Francis Campbell John Burns	Absconding with Union clothes	1st December 1853	Flogged
Mary Carroll	Refusing to work and damaging her clothes	8th November 1854	9 hours in lock-up
Mary Carroll	Persisting in refusing to work	9th November 1854	7 hours in lock-up

Above is a document from Newry workhouse. Read it and answer these questions:

1 In what county is Newry?

2 What book are these pages taken from?

3 Why was there a problem with discipline in the Newry workhouse?

4 What do you think a 'leathern taws' looked like?

5 Which punishment, in your opinion, was most severe?

6 Why do you think Mary Carroll refused to work and what was her punishment?

7 Francis Campbell and John Burns were flogged for trying to escape. Why do you think they tried?

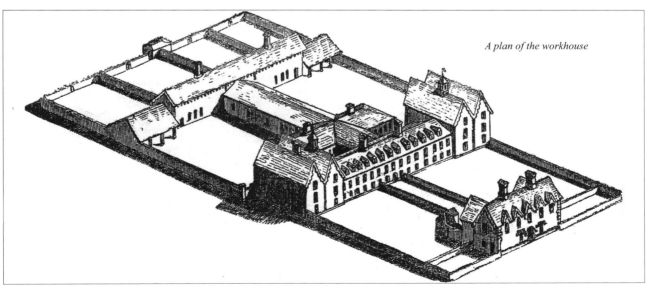

A plan of the workhouse

FOLK MEDICINE

Mary Kate gives the children cures to take with them on their journey: one for fever, one for stomach ache and cramps and another for cuts, wounds and stings.

Folk medicine has a long and respected tradition in Ireland. In many parts of rural Ireland there were people like Mary Kate who were said to have cures for certain human and animal ailments. Often the cures were passed on from one generation to another, or were known only to special people like the seventh son of a seventh son.

The cure could be a prayer, a particular sign or ritual, or the application of a special preparation made from local sources.

Lone thorn trees were thought to have healing powers. If a patient transferred a rag from around their ailment to the thorn tree the ailment was also transferred to the tree, and the patient was cured.

Certain wells were renowned for having healing properties. Usually these cures were obtained by drinking the water or by saying a prayer or leaving some object at the site. These places often became places of pilgrimage.

> 1 Check out the labels on shampoo and cosmetic containers.
> How many plants can you find in the list of ingredients?
>
> 2 What are they used for?
>
> 3 Sketch the plants with help from a reference book/disc.

HERE ARE SOME UNUSUAL CURES

- **For a stitch in the side** – rub the part affected with unsalted butter and make the sign of the cross seven times over the place.

- **For weak eyes** – a deconcoction of the flowers of daisies boiled down is an excellent wash to be used constantly.

- **For the mumps** – wrap the child in a blanket, take it to the pigsty, rub the child's head to the back of a pig and the mumps will leave it and pass from the child to the animal.

- **To cure warts** – on meeting a funeral, take some of the clay from under the feet of the men who bear the coffin and apply it to the wart, wishing strongly at the same time that it may disappear … and so it will be.

Lady Wilde, 1887

If you know any local cures e-mail them to us at: Channel 4 website: http://www.channel4.com/schools. Go to the Forum section and click on the *Under the Hawthorn Tree* topic.

Here is an example: In West Cavan chewing the leaf of a hawthorn used to be recommended as a cure for heartburn.

LANDLORDS

- Landlords were the most powerful people in the country, both economically and politically.
- They lived on the rent they got from their tenants and on the sale of their crops.
- It was from the landlord class that Members of Parliament were elected to Westminster. (There had been no Irish Parliament since the Act of Union in 1800.)
- The landlords contributed to the cost of the government Famine Relief Schemes through taxation.

1 Read and discuss the accounts below of people's memories of the landlords in their area – some good, some bad.

ORAL SOURCES

Michael Howard, b.1883, a farmer, Gladree, Belmullet, Co. Mayo

When the Famine of Black Forty-Seven was nearly over, and the most of the people of West Connaght were dead of cold and hunger, a man left Belmullet with his boat and went to England for a cargo of meal to try and save some of the lives of the poor people. This man was known as John Lally, who had owned a boat of his own, and was living in a small house in Belmullet. When this man came from England with his boatload of Indian meal to the pier at Belmullet, the landlords that were in Connaght at that time took

Conchubhair and Solomon Ó Néill, b.1860s, farmers, Cratloe, Co. Clare

One landlord (Lord George Quinn) cleared out several families in the townland of Ballymorris, for non-payment of rent.

Against this, Mr Maunsell (afterwards Lord Emly) gave seven pounds to each householder who left (1852 and for years after). If they remained he did not press them in any way, or leave a process at any man's door. Neither did he ask a vote from any of his tenants in O'Connell's time. He was elected MP for Limerick and also became a Catholic.

A landlord's residence

An enlightened Co. Limerick landlord, Thomas Spring-Rice

Séamus Reardon, b.1873, Boulteen, Eniskeane, Co. Cork

I must say they [the landlords] were not all alike. My grandfather, God rest his soul, went to pay part of his rent to his landlord, he was a Bantry man.

'Feed your family first, then give me what you can afford when times get better,' he told him.

So when times improved there was two years rent due on the majority of the small farms and very little hope of paying it later. This was a serious matter for the poor landlords. The rich landlords could afford to lose a little.

William (Bill) Powell, b. 1869, Eniskeane, Co. Cork

Yes, the famine was man-made. It was our rulers that saw to it that our food was shipped away to England from us, and left the people here starving.

Mrs Hanniffe, b. 1867, Kilkeaskin, Cairbre, Co. Kildare

Fifty families were evicted from this district of Kilkeaskin by a local landlord. The thatch of the roofs was torn off even before the poor people had time to leave.

ABSENTEE LANDLORDS

In *Under the Hawthorn Tree*, the local landlord, **Lord Edward Lyons, goes back to England and leaves his estate and the collection of rents in the hands of his agents, Jer Simmonds and Tom Daly.**

2 What effect do you think it had on an area if the landlord was an 'absentee landlord'?

EPISODE 4 – THE SEARCH

SUMMARY
The children are driven by hunger to seek food in the soup-kitchen. Later they come upon the body of a dead man and though horrified they respect the dead and say a prayer for him. They travel on, at times hungry, despondent and exhausted. Peggy is attacked by dogs and becomes feverish. Michael goes to the workhouse to get food but to no avail. He bleeds a cow and cooks the blood. Peggy recovers and eventually they reach Castletaggart and meet the great-aunts who, though poor themselves, accept them as part of the family. Eily has mixed emotions as she thinks back to the little thatched cottage and happier times.

BEFORE VIEWING
Ask the pupils to focus on the roles the children adopt. Is there boys' and girls' work, or do they cross over?

AFTER VIEWING
Summarise the episode and suggest that the pupils complete the character sketch begun in Worksheet No. 1. Ask them to write their last journal entry entitled: 'Journey's End'. Now they can assemble their four entries and a cover (see Worksheet No. 19).

WORKSHEET ACTIVITIES TABLE – AT A GLANCE

W/SHEET NO.	TITLE	ENGLISH	HISTORY	SPHE / PSHE	ART/MEDIA STUDIES	MUSIC
19	Cover Design				Book covers	
20	Boys' Work and Girls' Work	Letter writing, reading, discussing	Research working conditions	Gender stereotyping		
21	Soup-kitchens	Debate	Studying evidence/oblique sources	Proselytising /nutrition		
22	Death	Newspaper report	Contemporary accounts of starvation		Illustration for article	
23	Famine in Sudan, 1998		Deaths from famine - then and now	Current affairs		
24	Famine Song	Study of lyrics	Source material			Song
25	Endings	Creative writing/empathy				
26	Famine Quiz					

COVER DESIGN

HOW OTHERS SEE IT

On this page you can see actual covers from translations of *Under the Hawthorn Tree*.

1 You are to design the cover of a new edition of *Under the Hawthorn Tree*.
You will need to think about the following:

- What the story is about

- What the children look like and what they wear

- Which details you want on the cover

- What colour scheme suits the story.

2 Do some rough designs for your cover. Now select the best, improve on it and do a finished cover. Use it as a cover for your journal.

3 Hold a class or group discussion about the covers produced and compare with the covers from translations of *Under the Hawthorn Tree* reproduced on this page.

German (hardback)

Japanese

Dutch

German (paperback)

Swedish

French

Danish

BOYS' WORK AND GIRLS' WORK?

Before their mother leaves, she gives each of the children a function. This is what she said:

To Eily: 'You must take my place'
To Michael: 'The man of the house'
To Peggy: 'My baby'.

1 Look at the chart opposite and list what each of the children actually did in the circumstances listed in the left-hand column.

2 Their mother's expectation was that Michael would be the *hunter*, Eily the *carer* and Peggy the *object of affection*. Did they each fulfil that function or did they go beyond that stereotype? Discuss your findings and share your opinions with your classmates.

Life was harsh for all poor children during these times. If the O'Driscolls had been living in a large town or city, circumstances might have forced them to work:

❖ as servants in big houses
❖ down mines
❖ in factories
❖ making nails
❖ sweeping chimneys
❖ making ribbons.

3 Research what conditions would have been like for you if you had to work at one of these jobs. Write a letter to Queen Victoria complaining about these conditions and suggesting improvements.

WHAT THE CHILDREN ACTUALLY DID

EVENT	EILY	MICHAEL	PEGGY
Catching and cooking the rabbit			
Being attacked by dogs			
Peggy's fever			
Bleeding the cow			
The thunderstorm			
Robbing the orchard			

SOUP-KITCHENS

When the Government abandoned Public Works Schemes, public soup-kitchens were set up by government agencies and also by private institutions and by religious groups. In 1847 over 3 million people were receiving food. The Religious Society of Friends (Quakers) were especially notable for their generosity and courage in the face of sickness and fever. Other soup-kitchens were set up by over-zealous Protestant groups who demanded that people should abandon their Catholic faith in return for food. Those who converted were nicknamed 'Soupers'.

Quaker soup-kitchen, Cork

ORAL SOURCES

The Donegans, Ballintoy, Co. Antrim, in 1856
There was a soup-kitchen run by people named McKinnan in the townland of Cloughcur. They called them the 'Brockan-men'. It was porridge they would give if you would change your religion. At the time there was a lot of youngsters and these big people, the gentry, would take them to some place and give them food. The children would bless themselves before they would ate; and these ones would have their hands tied behind their backs so's they couldn't bless themselves. That happened round here as far as I heard.

Seán Ó Domhnaill, b.1873, Scairt na nGleobhrán, Ballylooby, Cahir, Co. Tipperary
Souperism was practised in the south-east of our parish so the tradition has it; and in the Ballybacon parish which is adjacent. To speak of a person as a 'Souper' in our district was tantamount to the greatest taunt and insult.

Lughaidh Ó Maollumhlaigh, Edgeworthstown, Co. Longford
Soup was given out by Protestant families who tried to get the people who took it to turn Protestant. Some did so.

A queue for soup

CLASS DEBATE
It was wrong to convert to get food.

DEATH

The children came upon the body of a man who died of disease or starvation at the side of the road. Out of respect for the dead, they said a prayer and marked the spot with a simple cross. During the famine many died in the same way without family, priest or coffin. Here are some accounts of the devastation caused by the famine.

ORAL SOURCES

Felix Kernan, b.1859, a farmer, Drumakill, Castleblayney, Co. Monaghan

When the potato crop failed no other food was available and the people perished by the hundreds of thousands, along the roadside, in the ditches, in the fields from hunger and cold, and what was even worse – the famine fever. The strongest men were reduced to mere skeletons and they could be met daily with the clothes hanging on them like ghosts.

The grandmother of the present writer often told me of her experiences when a girl of seventeen in those awful days. Her people had a little country shop and those customers who called on any particular day seldom or ever returned to the shop. She said it was usual to see corpses lying by the roadside with pieces of grass or leaves in their mouths and their faces stained with the juice of the plants which they were chewing to try and satisfy the hunger.

On one occasion a mother came in with a baby in her arms. The poor little thing was gaunt and thin and kept whining for something to eat. The mother would persist in putting its lips to her breasts which were milkless in order to stop it crying. A drink of milk was given to the baby and its mother and later the same day the mother was seen dead by the roadside with the baby still alive in her arms.

On another occasion a man called at the shop to buy a pound of meal to make porridge for his family of six. This small quantity of meal was boiled in a great deal of water to make more bulk but the thin gruel only hastened the end of the poor starving creatures and the next day four of them were dead in a neighbouring field.

John D. O'Leary, Lynedaowne, Rathmore, Co. Kerry

When I was a small boy I heard an old man talk of the Famine period. He said his mother sent him out to invite in a man that she saw leaning against a wall in Millstreet town. When he spoke the man did not answer. When he touched him he was dead.

When my grandmother (d.1894) was going to mass at Rathmore she saw a man lying dead on a heap of stones on the roadside. A young girl named Cotter is said to have died rather than accept help from the Soupers.

Dáithí Ó Ceanntabhail, national teacher, Croom, Co. Limerick

The deaths in my native place were many and horrible. The poor famine-stricken people were found by the wayside, emaciated corpses, partly green from eating docks and nettles and partly blue from the cholera and dysentery.

Tomás Ó Ceallaigh, b.1860, a farmer, Caherea, Ennis, Co. Clare

There was a labouring man in Caherea, his name was Cusack. He was found lying up against a wall dead in the morning. There was another man in Decomade and his name was Tom Hadlock. He was 18 years. He died of starvation. He was taken to Clondegad graveyard. They heard the noise in the coffin. They opened it and took him out and he lived to be an old man.

Select one of the extracts above. Make your own sketch based on that extract and below it write a contemporary report of the incident for the *Illustrated London News*. The year is 1847.

FAMINE IN SUDAN, 1998

Ireland 1848 – Sudan 1998

SUDAN FACTS

Area	2,376,000 Sq. Km. (largest in Africa)
Population	26.1 million (1994)
Head of State	General Omar al-Bashir
Capital	Khartoum, population 4 million
Language	Arabic, English, Local languages/dialects
Currency	Sudanese pound, S£90:US$1
GNP per capita	US$230 (Ireland's is US$16,061)
Exports	cotton, nuts, dates, gum arabic, sugar cane, sesame seed
Foreign Debt	US$21.5bn

NEWSPAPER EXTRACT –
The Irish Times, 2 June 1998

Paul Cullen reports on a visit to Bahr El Ghazal province in southern Sudan

We were halfway to the village of Malual Baai when we came across two women digging by the side of the road. The older woman, Aguek, explained what they were doing: 'The ants, they store away the grass seed under the ground, we know that. So we dig up their nest, and find the food.'

They had walked an hour from Malual Baai to get here at 6am and had collected about two cupfuls of seed by the time we arrived. Aguek explained that they would later crush this, remove the chaff, and then boil it to make a sort of soup.

'We have been eating wild foods but some of these are finished,' she explained, sipping some discoloured water from a gourd by her side.

Everywhere in this flat savannah where nothing grows, people said they had been living for months on a diet of wild fruits, leaves and little else.

HISTORY

Sudan is divided into two cultures, a Muslim north and a Christian south. It has a rich and ancient culture dating from 2300BC and has been under Arab rule since AD671. In 1899 it became part of the British Empire, then became independent in 1955. Civil war between the wealthier north and the poorer south followed for seventeen years.

In 1969 Colonel Jaafar el-Nimiery took power in a coup and ruled until 1985 when General al-Bashir took over. In 1983 civil war broke out again between the SPLA (Sudan People's Liberation Army) and government forces. Since then Sudan's economy has fallen apart.

Weather has not helped, and droughts and famine have occurred regularly since 1984.

CURRENT FOOD CRISIS

Prolonged fighting and drought in Bahr El Gazal, Nuba and Equatoria provinces have left thousands of people homeless and without food. Food stores are gone, seed crops have made it impossible to buy food. Over 350,000 people are in danger of starving. If no crop is sown, Sudan will be ravaged by famine and these people will die.

CLASS DISCUSSIONS

1 Based on the report above, how do you think the famine in the Sudan compares with the Irish famine?

2 Under the following topics, discuss the similarities and differences between Ireland in the last century and Sudan today: History, Religion, Area, Population, Language, Export, Land Ownership, Causes of Famine, Effects of Famine.

Further information from:

Concern, Camden Street, Dublin 2

Oxfam, 274 Banbury Road, Oxford, OX2 7DZ

Trocaire, 169 Booterstown Avenue, Blackrock, Co. Dublin

or other organisations you may know of.

EPISODE 4 – THE SEARCH

WORKSHEET 23

FAMINE SONG

Skibbereen

KEY Bm

Oh, father dear, I oft-times hear you talk of E-rin's Isle, Her
lof-ty scene and val-ley green, her moun-tains rude and wild, They
say it is a pret-ty place where-in a prince might dwell, Then
why did you a-ban-don it? The rea-son to me tell.

Oh, son, I loved our native land with energy and pride,
Until a blight came on the land and sheep and cattle died,
The rent and taxes were to pay, I could not them redeem,
And that's the cruel reason why I left old Skibbereen.

It's well I do remember that bleak December day.
The landlord and the sheriff came to drive us all away.
They set the roof on fire with their demon yellow spleen,
And that's another reason why I left old Skibbereen.

Your mother, too, God rest her soul, fell on the snowy ground.
She fainted in her anguish, seeing the desolation round.
She never rose, but passed away from life to mortal dream,
And found a quiet grave, my boy, in dear old Skibbereen.

It's well I do remember the year of forty-eight,
When I arose with Erin's boys to fight against the fate,
I was hunted through the mountains for a traitor to the queen,
And that's another reason why I left old Skibbereen.

Oh, father dear, the day may come when vengeance loud will call,
And we will rise with Erin's boys and rally one and all.
I'll be the man to lead the van beneath our flag of green,
When loud and high we'll raise the cry: 'Remember Skibbereen'.

Read the song and answer the questions.

1 There are two voices in this song. Identify them. Which verses belong to which character?

2 Is the son's view of Ireland realistic?

3 Describe the circumstances surrounding the father's departure from Skibbereen (key words: blight, rent, eviction, death).

4 What do you think happened to the son following the mother's death?

5 What do you think the cry 'Remember Skibbereen' meant to the son?

ENDINGS

1 Do you find the ending of the book and film satisfactory? Give reasons for your answer.

2 What do you think happened to the parents?

3 What might have happened if the great-aunts had rejected the children or been dead?

4 Do you think the children changed during the journey? Say how and why.

5 Do you think the changes will be permanent?

6 The final image is of Bridget's grave under the hawthorn tree with Mary Kate watching over it. What does that final scene make you think about?

WHAT HAPPENED NEXT?

7 Project the characters forward in time to the year 1866. Where are they now, twenty years on? Enter your suggestions on the chart below.

Where are they now?

Eily	
Michael	
Peggy	
Mary Kate	
Margaret (mother)	
John (father)	

THE FUTURE FOR EILY, MICHAEL, PEGGY

These two books are sequels to *Under the Hawthorn Tree*. Read how the author imagined the future lives of Eily, Michael and Peggy in the following years.

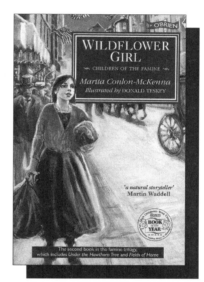

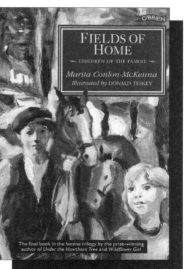

Compare your guesses about the children's future lives with the stories told in these books.

FAMINE QUIZ

1 In which decade of which century did the Great Famine occur?

2 What caused the famine?

3 What were weather conditions like that summer?

4 Why did the people not eat grain?

5 Why did they not buy food?

6 What did the Government import to feed the people?

7 What work was carried out under the Public Relief Schemes?

8 Where did the destitute go for food and shelter?

9 What diseases did the starving people contract?

10 What did the landlords do to help?

11 What were the free food distribution centres called?

12 To where did people emigrate?

13 How many people emigrated?

14 How many died?

15 What ended the famine?

Check your answers on pages 151-153 of Under the Hawthorn Tree.

ACKNOWLEDGEMENTS

Thanks to the following for permission to reproduce copyright material: The National Library of Ireland for illustrations on pp. 1, 7, 8 (and diet details), 9, 15 (top), 16, 19, 20, 21, 23, 26, 27, 28, 32; Ossian Publications Ltd., for 'Skibbereen', p.30; Faber & Faber Ltd., for the extract from 'Poet's Chair', Seamus Heaney, p.10; Concern for photographs, p.29 (photos taken by Liam Burke), and for Sudan Facts, p.29; *The Irish Times* for Kevin Myers article, p.10, and report on Sudan, p.29; The Georgian Society for engraving of Connolly's Folly, p.12; Gill and Macmillan for extracts from *Famine Echoes*, by Cathal Poirtéir, pp.16, 19, 23, 27, 28; The Deputy Keeper of the Records of Northern Ireland for extract from Newry Board of Guardians records, p.21; all film stills and extracts from screenplay were supplied by Young Irish Film Makers. Every effort has been made to contact copyright holders but if any oversight has occurred the publishers request the holders of such copyright to contact them.

Emigration after the famine

EPISODE 4 – THE SEARCH